PREPARED STATEMENT OF

THE FEDERAL TRADE COMMISSION

on

"Legislative Hearing on 17 FTC Bills"

Before the

COMMITTEE ON ENERGY AND COMMERCE

SUBCOMMITTEE ON COMMERCE, MANUFACTURING, AND TRADE

UNITED STATES HOUSE OF REPRESENTATIVES

Washington, D.C.

May 24, 2016

I.   INTRODUCTION

Doctor Burgess, Ranking Member Schakowsky, and members of the Subcommittee, I am

Edith Ramirez, Chairwoman of the Federal Trade Commission ("FTC" or "Commission").[1] I

appreciate the opportunity to present the Commission's testimony on the seventeen bills under

consideration by the Subcommittee. We appreciate this Subcommittee's commitment to

protecting both consumers and innovation.

The FTC is a highly productive and efficient, bipartisan independent agency with a broad

mission. It is the only federal agency with jurisdiction to both protect consumers and maintain

competition in most sectors of the economy. The agency enforces laws that prohibit business

practices that are unfair or deceptive to consumers, or anticompetitive, and seeks to do so

without impeding legitimate business activity.[2] The vast majority of our law enforcement

decisions are made unanimously.

The FTC also educates consumers and businesses to encourage informed consumer

choices, compliance with the law, and public understanding of the competitive process. In

addition, the FTC promotes consumer protection and competitive markets through its research,

advocacy, and policy work.

---

[1] This written statement presents the views of the Federal Trade Commission. My oral statements and responses to questions are my own and do not necessarily reflect the views of the Commission or of any other Commissioner.

[2] The FTC has broad law enforcement responsibilities under the Federal Trade Commission Act, 15 U.S.C. § 41 *et seq.*, and enforces a wide variety of other laws ranging from the Clayton Act to the Fair Credit Reporting Act. In total, the Commission has enforcement or administrative responsibilities under more than 70 laws. *See* http://www.ftc.gov/ogc/stats.shtm.

The impact of the FTC's work is significant. During the last fiscal year alone, the agency estimates that it saved consumers over $717 million through its consumer protection law enforcement actions and over $3.4 billion through its competition enforcement efforts.[3]

The FTC is committed to addressing the impact of technology and globalization as part of our law enforcement, rulemaking, and policy work. The Commission applies a balanced, fact-based approach to our law enforcement and other responsibilities. We work to enhance our understanding of how technology affects consumers and the functioning of the marketplace through research and engagement with industry, academic, and other experts. We have also deepened our internal technical expertise. We hired our first Chief Technologist in 2010 and have continued to attract prominent experts to serve in this role. Last year we created our Office of Technology Research and Investigation ("OTech") to support our law enforcement efforts and explore cutting-edge technical and policy issues relating to Big Data, the Internet of Things, and other emerging technologies.

But even as commerce and technology continue to evolve, many of the fundamental problems we see in the marketplace remain the same: consumer fraud schemes, deceptive advertising, unfair practices causing substantial consumer harm with little or no benefits to consumers or competition, as well as mergers and conduct that harm or threaten to harm competition. The agency tackles these challenges through targeted law enforcement. Our structure, research capacity, continued commitment to bipartisanship and cooperation, and committed staff enable the FTC to continue to meet its mandate of protecting consumers and competition in an ever-changing marketplace.

---

[3] *See* Summary of Performance and Financial Information Fiscal Year 2015 (Feb. 2016), *available at* https://www.ftc.gov/reports/ftc-fy-2015-summary-performance-financial-information.

II. THE SUBCOMMITTEE'S PROPOSED BILLS

The FTC appreciates the opportunity to comment on the seventeen proposed bills before the Subcommittee. While the Commission generally supports several of the bills, we believe that other measures may unintentionally hamper the FTC's ability to continue to fulfill its mission to protect consumers and competition.

A. Bills Addressing Specific Acts or Practices: Consumer Reviews, Made in the USA Labelling, Sports Equipment Concussion Claims, Online Hotel Reservations, Funeral Goods and Services, and Event Ticket Sales

House Bills 5111, 5092, 4460, 4526, 5212, 5245, and 5104, if enacted, would identify and address specific acts or practices that Congress proposes to include in the Commission's consumer protection agenda. The Commission has done significant work on most of these issues already, discussed in more detail below.

H.R. 5111, the Consumer Review Fairness Act, would help to prevent companies from silencing truthful consumer reviews of products and services – reviews that could help other consumers make important choices and potentially avoid harm. The FTC has used its existing authority to challenge companies that try to prevent consumers from sharing their truthful reviews online. In *Roca Labs*, for example, the FTC alleged the defendants not only promoted unproven weight loss supplements, but also threatened to sue consumers who shared their negative experiences online, claiming that the consumers violated the non-disparagement provisions of the company's "Terms and Conditions." [4] The FTC alleged that these gag clauses, and the defendants' related warnings, threats, and lawsuits, harmed consumers by unfairly barring purchasers from sharing truthful, negative comments about the defendants and their

---

[4] *FTC v. Roca Labs, Inc.*, No. 8:15-cv-02231-MSS-TBM (M.D. Fla. filed Sept. 28, 2015), *available at* https://www.ftc.gov/enforcement/cases-proceedings/142-3255/roca-labs-inc.

products. The bill would void such clauses in form contracts and deter their use by allowing the FTC to seek civil penalties for violations of the Consumer Review Fairness Act. The Commission welcomes these additional law enforcement tools.

House Bill 5092, the Reinforcing American-Made Products Act, would give the FTC exclusive authority to set and enforce the standard for when something can be labelled "Made in the USA" or with a similar claim. The Commission developed its standard of "all or virtually all" using evidence of consumer understanding, and has publicized this standard through enforcement actions, advisory opinions on particular products, and an enforcement policy statement.[5] The FTC also provides guidance to businesses on how they might comply with the standard and regularly works with companies making deceptive claims to help them come into compliance.[6] The FTC will continue its leadership on this issue. We think the bill would be stronger, however, if states also could challenge "Made In USA" claims applying the FTC's standard.

H.R. 4460, the Youth Sports Concussions Act, would give the FTC civil penalty authority, and authorize actions by states, to address the importation and sale of sports equipment for which the importer or seller has made deceptive safety benefit claims. The Commission shares the Subcommittee's concerns about deceptive concussion protection and other safety benefit claims for sports equipment. Claims that implicate serious health concerns – especially those potentially affecting children and young adults – are always a high priority for the

---

[5] *See Enforcement Policy Statement on U.S. Origin Claims*, 62 Fed. Reg. 63755 (Dec. 2, 1997), *available at* https://www.ftc.gov/public-statements/1997/12/enforcement-policy-statement-us-origin-claims.

[6] *Id. See also* FTC Guidance, *Selling 'American-Made' Products? What Businesses Need to Know About Making Made in USA Claims* (Oct. 2001), *available at* https://www.ftc.gov/tips-advice/business-center/guidance/selling-american-made-products-what-businesses-need-know-about; FTC Guidance, *Complying with the Made in USA Standard* (Dec. 1998), *available at* https://www.ftc.gov/tips-advice/business-center/guidance/complying-made-usa-standard.

Commission. Given the dangers that concussions and other injuries pose for athletes, it is essential that advertising for products claiming safety benefits be truthful and substantiated. Using its existing authority, the Commission has been active in this area. For example, in 2012, the agency settled allegations that mouthguard manufacturer Brain-Pad and its president made false and unproven claims that Brain-Pad mouthguards reduced the risk of concussions.[7] Following that case, the FTC sent warning letters to almost thirty sports equipment manufacturers and five retailers, advising them of the case and warning them that they also might be making deceptive concussion protection claims.[8] The agency also investigated three major football helmet manufacturers – Riddell Sports, Schutt Sports, and Xenith – in connection with their claims that their helmets reduced the risk of concussions. In these matters, the staff closed the investigations without taking formal action, by which time all three companies had discontinued potentially deceptive claims from their advertising or had agreed to do so.[9] H.R. 4460 would provide additional tools to protect consumers from such claims.

The Commission also shares concerns about deceptive online travel sites. H.R. 4526, the Stop Online Booking Scams Act, requires disclosures in order to prevent online travel sites from

---

[7] *Brain-Pad, Inc.*, No. C-4375 (Nov. 29, 2012), *available at* https://www.ftc.gov/enforcement/cases-proceedings/122-3073/brain-pad-inc.

[8] See, e.g., FTC Press Release, FTC Alerts Major Retailers to Concerns About Concussion Protection Claims for Athletic Mouthguards Made on Websites, Aug. 21, 2014, available at https://www.ftc.gov/news-events/press-releases/2014/08/ftc-alerts-major-retailers-concerns-about-concussion-protection.

[9] Copies of the staff's closing letters to the three companies are posted on the Commission's website. *See* Letter from Mary K. Engle to John E. Villafranco, Esq. (Apr. 24, 2013), *available at* https://www.ftc.gov/sites/default/files/documents/closing_letters/riddell-sports-group-inc./130430riddellvillafrancoltr.pdf; Letter from Mary K. Engle to Michael E. Antalics, Esq. (Apr. 24, 2013), *available at* https://www.ftc.gov/sites/default/files/documents/closing_letters/schutt-sports-inc./130430schuttatalicsltr.pdf; Letter from Mary K. Engle to Sheryl M. Bourbeau, Esq. (Apr. 24, 2013), *available at* https://www.ftc.gov/sites/default/files/documents/closing_letters/xenith-llc/130430xenithbourbeaultr.pdf.

deceiving consumers about their affiliation with hotels. However, we recommend modifying the bill to ensure that it does not impose undue burdens on legitimate businesses or unintentionally exclude the types of sites it intends to capture. Mainstream third-party online travel agencies generally do not generate the kind of deception addressed by the bill; for this reason, we recommend that rather than requiring all companies to make disclosures, the bill prohibit sales by those entities that misrepresent that they are affiliated with a hotel.

The FTC shares the Subcommittee's interest in ensuring consumers are protected against unfair or deceptive practices in connection with the provision of funeral goods and funeral services. Since the 1980s, the Funeral Industry Practices Trade Regulation Rule ("Funeral Rule"),[10] has been the centerpiece of the Commission's consumer protection law enforcement efforts in the industry. The Funeral Rule requires that costs and information be disclosed to consumers to enable them to make informed purchasing decisions at a time of extraordinary stress. Under the Commission's enforcement approach, which includes an industry self-regulatory system with Commission oversight, there appears to be a good level of compliance with the Rule. We note that aspects of H.R. 5212 enter upon areas historically within the purview of states and local municipalities.

The Commission supports the goal of H.R. 5245, the Better Oversight of Secondary Sales and Accountability in Concert Ticketing Act of 2016, which would require more transparency in ticket sales. The Commission recommends several changes, however, to better achieve that goal. To reduce consumer confusion from ineffective or excessive disclosures, the bill should prohibit misrepresentations that a secondary ticket seller is the venue or the primary ticket seller (rather than requiring disclosures) and should not require that secondary sellers disclose

---

[10] 16 C.F.R. Part 453.

distribution method, date, and time of purchase. Finally, the Commission recommends that the statutory requirements be specific enough to be enforced without a rule and that any rulemaking provision be discretionary rather than mandatory.

Finally, H.R. 5104, the Better On-line Ticket Sales Act, seeks to ensure that consumers, and not just scalpers with specialized software, can purchase online tickets to events such as concerts. As more and more ticket sales move online, consumers should not be excluded from opportunities to purchase them directly from the seller at face value.[11] At the same time, liability for selling software used for scalping should only be imposed for sales of specialized software designed for that purpose. Browsers, operating systems, and other general purpose software that scalpers might use in the process of circumventing ticket seller controls should not be covered because there should not be liability for the normal use of such beneficial, widely used software, and we recommend that the bill be modified to ensure this.

B. Bills that Would Expand the FTC's Jurisdiction

House Bills 5239 and 5255 would repeal certain exemptions to the FTC Act. The Commission supports repealing these exemptions to protect consumers and competition more broadly and to ensure consistent application of laws across economic sectors.

---

[11] The FTC has challenged companies that use deceptive claims and tactics to resell tickets. *See, e.g.*, *FTC v. TicketNetwork, Inc. et al.*, No. 3:14-cv-1046 (D. Conn. filed July 23, 2014), *available at* https://www.ftc.gov/enforcement/cases-proceedings/132-3203-132-3204-132-3207/ticketnetwork-inc-ryadd-inc-secureboxoffice (alleging that defendants' advertisements and websites misled consumers into thinking they were buying event tickets from the original venue at face value, when defendants' websites actually were ticket reseller sites with event tickets often priced above the venue's original price); *FTC v. Ticketmaster, LLC et al.*, No. 10-CV-01093 (N.D. Ill. filed Feb. 18, 2010), *available at* https://www.ftc.gov/enforcement/cases-proceedings/092-3091/ftc-v-ticketmaster-llc-limited-liability-company-ticketmaster (alleging Ticketmaster and its affiliates used deceptive bait-and-switch tactics to sell event tickets to consumers, often at much higher prices than face value and in some cases speculatively).

The Protecting Consumers in Commerce Act of 2016 would strike the telecommunications common carrier exception from the FTC Act, which bars the agency from reaching certain conduct by telecommunications companies.[12] The FTC has long called for the repeal of the common carrier exception, which originated in an era when telecommunications services were provided by highly-regulated monopolies. This is no longer true in the current marketplace, where firms frequently compete in providing telecommunications services and are less regulated.

As the telecommunications and Internet industries continue to converge, the common carrier exception is likely to frustrate the FTC's ability to stop deceptive and unfair acts and practices and unfair methods of competition with respect to a wide array of activities in the Internet and telecommunications industries. For example, because the FCC has reclassified broadband Internet access service as a common carriage service,[13] the provision of broadband is now not subject to FTC enforcement. Unless the common carrier exception is repealed, the Commission will not be able to bring in the future cases like the actions against AT&T[14] and TracFone.[15] In both cases, we alleged that the companies promised their customers unlimited data but in reality severely limited data usage by reducing – or throttling – the data speeds of

---

[12] 15 U.S.C. § 45(a)(2) excepts from the FTC Act "common carriers subject to the Acts to Regulate Commerce." 15 U.S.C. § 44 defines the "Acts to regulate commerce" as "Subtitle IV of Title 49 (interstate transportation) and the Communications Act of 1934" and all amendments thereto.

[13] *See In re Protecting and Promoting the Open Internet*, FCC 15-24 (2015) (report and order) (GN Docket No. 14-28).

[14] *FTC v. AT&T Mobility, Inc.*, No. 14-cv-04785-EMC (N.D. Cal. filed Oct. 28, 2014) (order denying motion to dismiss), *available at* https://www.ftc.gov/enforcement/cases-proceedings/122-3253/att-mobility-llc-mobile-data-service, appeal docketed, Case No. 15-16585 (9th Cir. Aug. 10, 2015).

[15] *FTC v. TracFone Wireless, Inc.*, No. 3:15-cv-00392 (N.D. Cal. filed Jan. 28, 2015), *available at* https://www.ftc.gov/enforcement/cases-proceedings/132-3176/straight-talk-wireless-tracfone-wireless-inc.

high-usage customers to the point that many common mobile phone applications, like web browsing, GPS navigation, and streaming video, became difficult or nearly impossible to use.

This type of basic consumer protection issue falls squarely within the core mission of the FTC. Such matters are emerging with increasing regularity in the telecommunications industry. Yet the common carrier exception may prevent the FTC from protecting consumers from these problems and emerging issues presented by new technologies and the blurring of industries.

Removing the exception from the FTC Act would enable the FTC to bring its extensive law enforcement experience to bear in protecting consumers of common carriage services against unfair and deceptive practices in the same way that it can protect against unfair and deceptive practices for other services. For example, we have a long history of privacy and data security enforcement against a wide range of entities under our jurisdiction that operate in the technology and communications industries – companies like Microsoft, Facebook, Google, HTC, and Twitter, app providers like Snapchat, Fandango, and Credit Karma, and cases involving the Internet of Things, mobile payments, retail tracking, crowdsourcing, and lead generators.

Although the FCC would retain its jurisdiction over common carriers, consumers would benefit from the FTC having shared jurisdiction because the enforcement provisions of the FTC Act provide for consumer redress. Whereas the FCC traditionally has exercised its authority to fine companies for noncompliance, the FTC focuses on putting money back in the pockets of consumers. For example, as part our settlement with TracFone, we returned $40 million to consumers. And, as part of our case alleging unlawful mobile cramming practices against T-Mobile, which we settled jointly with the FCC and all 50 states, we obtained $90 million for consumer redress. The FCC obtained $4.5 million in penalties.[16]

---

[16] *See* FTC Press Release, *T-Mobile to Pay At Least $90 Million, Including Full Consumer Refunds To*

The Commission also supports H.R. 5255, which would subject charitable, religious, educational and other nonprofit organizations to the FTC Act. Currently the FTC's jurisdiction over non-profits is limited.[17] The FTC Act applies to "persons, partnerships, or corporations,"[18] and the Act defines "corporation" as an entity that "is organized to carry on business for its own profit or that of its members."[19]

We support extension of our jurisdiction to certain non-profit entities. In healthcare provider markets, where the Commission has long sought to maintain competition, the agency's inability to reach conduct by various non-profit entities has prevented the Commission from taking action against potentially anticompetitive behavior of non-profits engaged in business.[20] These concerns also apply to our consumer protection mission. For example, despite many publicized data breaches at hospitals and universities, the FTC cannot challenge unfair or

---

Settle FTC Mobile Cramming Case, Dec. 19, 2014, *available at* https://www.ftc.gov/news-events/press-releases/2014/12/t-mobile-pay-least-90-million-including-full-consumer-refunds.

[17] The Commission has jurisdiction over most non-profits in several discrete areas, for example, under certain consumer financial statutes such as the Truth in Lending Act and the Equal Credit Opportunity Act. The Commission also has jurisdiction over non-profit entities for purposes of the Clayton Act, most notably Section 7, which prohibits mergers or acquisitions where "the effect of such acquisition may be substantially to lessen competition, or to tend to create a monopoly." 15 U.S.C. § 18.

[18] 15 U.S.C. § 45(a)(2).

[19] 15 U.S.C. § 44. Under this framework, the Commission can reach "sham" non-profits, such as shell non-profit corporations that actually operate for profit; for-profit entities falsely claiming to be affiliated with charitable organizations who affirmatively misrepresent that "donations" collected will go to charity; and organizations such as trade associations that engage in activities that provide substantial economic benefit to their for-profit members, for example, by providing advice and other arrangements on insurance and business matters, or engaging in lobbying activities.

[20] For example, the Commission generally cannot challenge anticompetitive conduct, such as collusive behavior, by non-profit hospitals. In three past enforcement actions, the Commission alleged that groups of physicians and hospitals had participated in unlawful price-fixing arrangements, but sued only the physicians and a for-profit hospital. *See Piedmont Health Alliance*, 138 F.T.C. 675 (2004) (consent order), *available at* https://www.ftc.gov/enforcement/cases-proceedings/0210119i/piedmont-health-alliance-inc-et-al-matter; *Tenet Healthcare Corp./Frye Regional Medical Center*, 137 F.T.C. 219 (2004) (consent order), *available at* https://www.ftc.gov/enforcement/cases-proceedings/0210119h/tenet-healthcare-corporation-frye-regional-medical-center-inc; *Maine Health Alliance*, 136 F.T.C. 616 (2003) (consent order), *available at* https://www.ftc.gov/enforcement/cases-proceedings/0210017/maine-health-alliance-william-r-diggins-matter.

deceptive data security or privacy practices of these entities.[21] These breaches have exposed the sensitive data of millions of consumers, yet the Commission cannot act due to the non-profit status of these entities. Further, while the Commission can use Section 5 to reach "sham" non-profits, such as shell non-profit corporations that actually operate for profit[22] and sham charities,[23] each such investigation requires resource-intensive factfinding to satisfy this standard.

C.   Bills that Could Facilitate FTC Deliberations and Highlight Important Work

The Commission supports H.R. 5116, the Freeing Responsible and Effective Exchange Act, as well as portions of H.R. 5098, the FTC Robust Elderly Protections and Organizational Requirements to Track Scams Act. The FTC is committed to providing transparency of its operations, but appreciates the Committee's efforts in H.R. 5116 to give a bipartisan majority of Commissioners another way in which to meet and deliberate. Although these meetings would need to comply with certain conditions that do not apply under the current Sunshine Act, the bill would allow a bipartisan group of at least three Commissioners to close meetings that would otherwise have to be open. Such meetings would enable the Commissioners to confer and advance the work of the agency. As the Committee continues to consider this measure, the Commission asks that it ensure that H.R. 5116 provides a mechanism in addition to, rather than in lieu of, the existing Sunshine Act procedures.

---

[21] A substantial number of reported breaches have involved non-profit universities and health systems. *See* Privacy Rights Clearinghouse Chronology of Data Breaches (listing breaches including breaches at non-profits, educational institutions, and health facilities), *available at* http://www.privacyrights.org/data-breach/new.

[22] *See, e.g., FTC v. Ameridebt, Inc.*, 343 F. Supp. 2d 451, 460-62 (D. Md. 2004) (denying motion to dismiss where FTC complaint alleged that purported credit counseling organization incorporated as a non-profit entity was a "de facto for-profit organization"). The history of the FTC's case is available at https://www.ftc.gov/enforcement/cases-proceedings/0223171/ameridebt-inc.

[23] *See, e.g., FTC et al. v. Cancer Fund of America, Inc. et al.*, No. CV15-884 PHX NVW (D. Az. filed May 19, 2015), *available at* https://www.ftc.gov/enforcement/cases-proceedings/122-3005-x150042/cancer-fund-america-inc.

The FTC also supports the call in H.R. 5098 for an annual report to Congress on elder

fraud, though we would recommend broadening the report to capture all of what the FTC is

doing on behalf of seniors. Combatting fraud is a critical component of the FTC's consumer

protection mission. Our research shows that older Americans are not necessarily defrauded at

higher rates than younger consumers, and that current threats to seniors include a wide array of

frauds that affect the American population broadly.[24] However, certain types of scams are more

likely to impact older Americans, such as technical support imposter schemes or scams relating

to health care. As the population of older Americans grows rapidly, the FTC's efforts to

recognize trends that affect them, bring aggressive law enforcement action, and educate seniors

become increasingly vital.[25]

The Commission has taken a multi-faceted approach that encompasses robust law

enforcement against scams that both target and impact seniors, strategic policy proposals, and

vigorous consumer education and outreach. For example, *Pass It On* is our most recent

education effort aimed at people who are 65 and older.[26] The *Pass It On* program is specifically

designed for seniors so they educate themselves and others about consumer protection issues.

Expanding the scope of H.R. 5098 to include *all* of the Commission's efforts in an annual report

to Congress would provide a more complete and accurate description of the important work we

---

[24] The FTC's third consumer fraud survey revealed that the overall rate of victimization for consumers 65 and older was significantly lower than for younger consumers. Fed. Trade Comm'n Bureau of Economics Staff Report, *Consumer Fraud in the U.S., 2011*, at 56-59 (Apr. 2013), *available at* https://www.ftc.gov/reports/consumer-fraud-united-states-2011-third-ftc-survey.

[25] In its 2014 report, the U.S. Census Bureau stated that by 2050, it projects the population over 65 to be 83.7 million, nearly double the estimated population of 43.1 million in 2012. By 2030, the U.S. Census Bureau also anticipates that more than 20 percent of U.S. residents will be over the age of 65, compared to 13 percent in 2010 and 9.8 percent in 1970. *See* Jennifer Ortman, Victoria Velkoff, & Howard Hogan, U.S. Department of Commerce, U.S. Census Bureau, An Aging Nation: The Older Population in the United States, at 1-3 (May 2014), *available at* https://www.census.gov/prod/2014pubs/p25-1140.pdf.

[26] *See* www.ftc.gov/passiton and www.ftc.gov/pasalo.

do in this area. FTC staff would be happy to provide technical assistance to the Subcommittee to modify the bill to do this.

D.   FTC Process Reform Measures

The FTC recognizes and supports the goals of the remaining bills: the avoidance of undue burdens on business; transparency of agency operations and its application of the law; and assurance that agency actions are based on sound analysis and evidence. In fact, the agency already has a variety of processes in place to advance these important values. We are concerned, however, that the measures could have the unintended effect of impairing protection of consumers and competition.

1.   *Avoiding Undue Burdens on Businesses*

We share the Subcommittee's goal of avoiding undue burdens on businesses. An important part of the FTC's mission is to protect consumers without impeding legitimate business activity. The importance of this mandate is heightened by the potential for new technology to transform markets. Two of the bills under consideration – H.R.5093, the Technological Innovation through Modernizing Enforcement Act, and H.R. 5097, the Start Taking Action on Lingering Liabilities Act – seek to address this. However, the Commission already has procedures in place to address these concerns in a flexible manner that still allows the Commission to protect consumers effectively.

H.R. 5093, the Technological Innovation through Modernizing Enforcement Act, for example, would place an eight-year time limit on most administrative consent orders, in an attempt to make sure they do not impair technological innovation. It would apply to both the FTC's consumer protection and competition cases, and would allow for only limited exceptions for consent orders "relate[d] to alleged fraud."[27] The legislation would prevent the Commission

from entering longer consent orders when necessary and appropriate to protect competition and

consumers from acts and practices that violate laws enforced by the FTC.[28] It also would remove

the flexibility the Commission currently has to modify or terminate any consent order when

appropriate, which may also harm companies currently under order.

Existing law, rules, and practices already provide flexibility for the Commission to enter

into, and modify or terminate, consent orders. Commission administrative consent orders

generally sunset after 20 years.[29] The Commission can and has agreed to shorter terms for

specific provisions within orders, when appropriate.[30] And, under Section 5(b) of the FTC Act,

parties can seek modification of consent orders at any time upon a satisfactory showing of

changed conditions of law or fact that warrant changing the order.[31] Under the bill, however,

---

[27] Even for consent orders "relate[d] to alleged fraud," the bill would restrict the Commission from entering into a consent order lasting longer than eight years unless the Commission first considers: (1) the impact of technological progress on the continuing relevance of an order, and (2) whether, as of the date the order is entered, there is reason to believe that the entity would resume the prohibited conduct eight years later.

[28] The proposed language also would create a significant disparity between permanent injunctions issued by federal courts pursuant to Section 13(b) of the FTC Act and the Commission's administrative consent orders.

[29] *See* 60 Fed. Reg. 42569 (Aug. 16, 1995). The Commission concluded that administrative orders ordinarily fulfill their remedial purposes within 20 years, and therefore they should ordinarily terminate after 20 years.

[30] For example, in its data security cases against Twitter and Dave & Buster's, the Commission required the companies to obtain biannual security assessments, but only for 10 years, not the full 20 year duration of the orders. *See Twitter, Inc.*, No. C-4316 (Mar. 11, 2011), *available at* https://www.ftc.gov/enforcement/cases-proceedings/092-3093/twitter-inc-corporation; *Dave & Buster's, Inc.*, No. C-4291 (June 8, 2010), *available at* https://www.ftc.gov/enforcement/cases-proceedings/082-3153/dave-busters-incin-matter. The FTC also often shortens certain order provisions, such as those that require recordkeeping and reporting, to periods significantly less than 20 years. Similarly, the key provisions in Commission orders requiring divestitures to remedy the likely effects of an anticompetitive merger are executed quickly, often within ten days. Where the respondent has additional obligations to provide services in aid of the buyer, these provisions last only as long as is necessary to ensure the buyer is able to compete effectively on its own – usually no longer than three years.

[31] *E.g.*, *Nine West Group, Inc.*, 145 F.T.C. 351 (2008), *available at* https://www.ftc.gov/sites/default/files/documents/cases/2008/05/080506order.pdf (2008) (modifying a

parties can seek only to terminate an order, and can do so only for certain orders, and only after the orders have been in place for five years.

The Commission's past work demonstrates the frequent need to protect consumers through consent orders that go beyond an eight-year timeframe. The FTC has brought at least 10 district court enforcement actions for violations of consent orders that were over 15 years old and that involved serious, recurring violations.[32] For example, the Commission enforced its order against Dahlberg, Inc. in 1995 alleging violations of the 1976 order based on false and unsubstantiated claims for its Miracle-Ear "Clarifier," a "noise-suppression" hearing aid.[33]

H.R. 5097, the Start Taking Action on Lingering Liabilities Act, would automatically terminate investigations if the Commission does not send the company being investigated a "verifiable" written communication every six months, or vote to continue the investigation. Like H.R. 5093, it is intended to relieve businesses of a burden – uncertainty about whether an FTC investigation is still open – but may impede the Commission's ability to protect consumers without adding corresponding benefits. In particular, Commission rules already incentivize staff to engage in ongoing communications with entities subject to an investigation. If a company subject to an access letter, Commission compulsory process, or a demand to preserve material

---

2000 consent order concerning resale price maintenance); *Beneficial Corp.*, 108 F.T.C. 168 (1986) (modifying a 1979 consent order concerning advertising of tax preparation services); *Kroger Co.*, 113 F.T.C. 772 (1990) (modifying a 1977 consent order concerning unavailability of food products).

[32] *See, e.g.*, *United States v. KB Home*, No. 91-0872 WQH (POR) (S.D. Cal Modified Consent Decree filed Aug. 3, 2005), *available at* https://www.ftc.gov/enforcement/cases-proceedings/united-states-america-plaintiff-v-kb-home-previously-kaufman-broad-inc (alleging violations of an order issued in 1979 by including arbitration clauses in warranties that were binding upon the consumer); *United States v. General Nutrition, Inc.*, No. 94-0686 (W.D. Pa. Consent Decree May 20, 1994), *available at* https://www.ftc.gov/enforcement/cases-proceedings/general-nutrition-corporation-also-trading-natural-sales-company-david (alleging violations of orders issued in 1969 and 1989 by misrepresenting the efficacy of dietary supplements).

[33] *United States v. Dahlberg, Inc.*, No. 4-94-CV-165 (D. Minn. Consent Decree filed Nov. 21, 1995), *available at* https://www.ftc.gov/news-events/press-releases/1995/11/ftc-settles-false-advertising-charges-against-maker-miracle-ear.

does not receive a written communication from FTC staff within twelve months, the company's duty to preserve the material expires.[34] And, while agency staff strives to maintain ongoing communications with entities under investigation, H.R. 5097 could result in the automatic termination of important investigations due to lost mail or a procedural oversight.

2.   *Providing Enforcement and Operational Transparency*

The Commission, like the Subcommittee, believes in the critical importance of transparency. However, H.R. 5109, H.R. 5118, and portions of H.R. 5098 may have unintended adverse effects and could also undermine the FTC's ability to perform its mission efficiently, effectively, and fairly.

H.R. 5109, the Clarifying Legality and Enforcement Action Reasoning Act, would require the FTC to publish an annual report to Congress on its consumer protection investigations, describing both those that result in agency action as well as those that are closed. All Commission investigations that result in agency action are already made public through press releases, which summarize each action and provide links to additional information. It would further require a report describing these actions. For companies against whom the FTC did not take formal action, the Commission would have to report the legal basis for closing the investigation and the industry sector in which the company under investigation operated. Such a requirement would risk harming the reputation of these companies. Entities investigated by the FTC often do not want investigations disclosed due to a concern that it would affect their reputations and possibly invite follow-on litigation. Although the intent of H.R. 5109 is not to reveal the identity of the person being investigated, the requirement that the Commission provide

---

[34] 16 C.F.R. § 2.14.

its legal analysis and specify the industry sector in each matter would, in many instances, make it easy to identify the company.

The Commission understands the value of explaining its views and analysis to guide businesses in their practices, and already does this in many different ways. The FTC communicates what it believes to be unfair or deceptive acts or practices through published opinions or statements in litigated or settled cases; press releases; annual reports; meetings with outside parties; outreach to business groups and trade associations; testimony to Congress; a website devoted to business education; and formal and informal guidance, including events throughout the country and online materials such as business blogs. In addition, whenever staff closes a matter, it considers whether to publish a closing letter as a means of providing industry additional guidance.

Also concerning is the amount of work that producing the case summaries called for in the bill would entail, and the significant opportunity costs of doing this. Last year, for example, the Commission closed over 250 investigations, many of them without formal action. A substantial number of these matters were closed for fact-specific reasons – including trade secrets or other confidential business information that the FTC may be barred by statute from disclosing[35] – and an explication of these cases would shed little light on how the Commission might apply the law in other circumstances.

Similarly, in addition to requiring a report on fraud targeted at seniors, H.R. 5098, the FTC Robust Elderly Protections and Organizational Requirements to Track Scams Act, would require an annual report to Congress on its plans for the upcoming year. We are happy to

---

[35] The FTC may not publicly disclose trade secrets, commercial or financial information, or any other information or materials submitted pursuant to or in lieu of compulsory process that the respondent marks as confidential. 15 U.S.C. § 46(f), 57b-2.

17

continue to keep the Subcommittee apprised of Commission activities, but are concerned that requiring additional reporting of the agency's plans would impair the FTC's ability to respond to emergent issues, or would not produce helpful additional information. The Commission already reports considerable information about its plans and operations.[36] For example, pursuant to the Government Performance and Results Act of 1993 and the GPRA Modernization Act of 2010, the FTC already publishes a Strategic Plan at the beginning of each new term of an Administration. The Strategic Plan provides a road map of objectives, strategies, and performance goals that will guide the agency's work.[37] Every year, the Commission also publishes and submits to Congress as part of its Congressional Budget Justification accompanying the President's budget request, an Annual Performance Plan for the current and following fiscal years, along with an Annual Performance Report for the preceding fiscal year.[38] In addition, every spring the Chairwoman issues an Annual Highlights Report that briefly describes FTC programs and accomplishments in its missions of protecting consumers and promoting competition.[39] The Commission also provides information to the public about its comprehensive rule review program and any other regulatory activity by publishing a ten-year rule review schedule every year, and a regulatory agenda semi-annually.[40]

---

[36] *See generally* https://www.ftc.gov/about-ftc/performance.

[37] *See, e.g.*, FTC, Strategic Plan for Fiscal Years 2014 to 2018, *available at* https://www.ftc.gov/reports/2014-2018-strategic-plan.

[38] *See, e.g.*, FY 2016-2017 Performance Plan and FY 2015 Performance Report, *available at* https://www.ftc.gov/reports/fy-2016-2017-performance-plan-fy-2015-performance-report-0.

[39] *See, e.g.*, *FTC Annual Highlights 2015*, *available at* https://www.ftc.gov/reports/annual-highlights-2015.

[40] *See, e.g.*, 16 CFR Part 1: Notice of Intent to Request Public Comments Concerning the Federal Trade Commission's Modified Ten-Year Regulatory Review Schedule (Feb. 16, 2016), *available at* https://www.ftc.gov/policy/federal-register-notices/16-cfr-part-1-notice-intent-request-public-comments-concerning-0. The FTC reviews its rules and industry guides on a 10-year schedule to ensure they stay relevant and are not overly burdensome. The review schedule is published each year, with adjustments in response to public input, changes in the marketplace, and resource demands. Also, in accordance with

And, to get the word out about its workshops, conferences, and studies, the FTC uses numerous channels, including its website, press releases, social media, email lists, and partners, among others. In 2015, for example, the FTC added over 64,000 email subscribers to its notifications, bringing the total number of email subscribers to almost 250,000 recipients.

Another bill, H.R. 5118, the Solidifying Habitual and Institutional Explanations of Liability and Defenses Act, provides that the FTC may not base an enforcement action solely on the acts or practices that are alleged to be inconsistent with guidance or similar statements, but that a company may use compliance with guidance as evidence of compliance with the law. The Commission's existing Rule on the Application of Guides in Preventing Unlawful Practices makes it clear that Commission guides are only an administrative interpretation of the law designed to assist businesses in complying.[41] The Commission will take action against an entity engaging in conduct that does not comply with the guide only if it has reason to believe that the specific conduct at issue violates the law itself. Under the FTC's Rule 1.3 on requesting advisory opinions, the Commission will not proceed against a party that has received guidance with respect to any action taken in good faith reliance on the Commission's advice. The bill, however, makes compliance with guidance constitute compliance with the law itself – thus substituting the guidance for the law and precluding the Commission from considering the law's

---

section 22(d) of the FTC Act (15 U.S.C. § 57b-3) and in keeping with the goals of sections 4(b)-(c) of Executive Order 12,866, the FTC publishes a semi-annual regulatory agenda that identifies and describes its plans for the upcoming year's rulemaking activities, including identifying any forthcoming proposed or final rules that are likely to have a significant economic impact on small entities, as well as an annual regulatory plan that describes the most important significant regulatory and deregulatory actions that the agency reasonably expects to issue in proposed or final form during the upcoming year. *See, e.g.,* FTC, Semiannual Regulatory Agenda (Nov. 19, 2015), *available at* https://resources.regulations.gov/public/ContentViewer?objectId=0900006481d7136e&disposition=attachment&contentType=pdf; Regulatory Information Service Center, Introduction to the Unified Agenda of Federal Regulatory and Deregulatory Actions, 80 Fed. Reg. 77710, 77903-11 (Dec. 15, 2015).

[41] *See* 16 C.F.R. Part 17.

applicability to the specific facts and circumstances of the case. If guidance were to

automatically become a safe harbor, this might chill the Commission's efforts to provide many

types of guidance to businesses, which have been highly effective. In 2015 alone, the agency

hosted 20 workshops on competition and consumer protection topics; issued 15 reports;

published 40 blog posts on competition topics and 143 consumer protection blog posts for

business people and attorneys; and added thousands of new email and social media followers.[42]

Almost 50,000 people subscribe to the Commission's business blog. And last year, consumers

and business people ordered more than 17 million copies of the FTC's print publications and

viewed 48.4 million pages of FTC information online. This guidance benefits both consumers

and businesses by facilitating and thus increasing compliance with the law.

3. *Ensuring Agency Actions Are Based on Sound Analysis and Evidence*

Finally, like the Subcommittee, the FTC believes in the importance of having sound legal

and economic bases for its actions. However, the Commission is concerned that H.R. 5136, the

Revealing Economic Conclusions for Suggestions Act, and H.R. 5115, the Statement on

Unfairness Reinforcement and Emphasis Act, may have the unintended consequence of

impairing the Commission's ability to stop harmful practices and provide meaningful

recommendations.

H.R. 5136 would require that, before the Commission could make a recommendation for

legislative or regulatory action, the Bureau of Economics ("BE") must provide an economic

analysis of the costs and benefits of such actions, as well as the ability of private markets or other

public institutions to address the issue in the absence of such action. Under the Commission's

---

[42] *See generally* Annual Highlights 2015, *available at* https://www.ftc.gov/reports/annual-highlights-2015.

current structure and practice, BE is integrally involved in almost everything the Commission does, providing Commission and staff with thorough, objective, and independent analyses. The FTC's comments on regulation and legislation, as well as its other activities, already are informed by BE's work. However, the type of comprehensive economic analysis imposed by the bill would both exceed BE's resources and require an economic analysis of factors well beyond competition and consumer protection.

By barring issuance of recommendations without such an analysis, the bill could prevent the FTC from providing: recommendations to Congress; comments on other agencies' proposals; suggestions for industry self-regulation; responses to state law makers seeking guidance on the competitive effects of proposed state bills; assistance to foreign governments seeking help in drafting competition and consumer protection laws; and aid in the development of best practice standards in multinational bodies, including those aimed at ensuring due process in antitrust cases. These are matters on which the agency may have expertise to contribute but is neither responsible for the ultimate decision nor necessarily expert as to the entire issue.

Also with the apparent goal of ensuring a sound basis for agency actions, H.R. 5115 would codify portions of the Commission's Unfairness Statement[43] into Section 5 of the FTC Act to ensure that FTC enforcement actions address only "substantial harm." The Unfairness Statement has helped focus the Commission's actions, and Congress's previous codification of the statement's principles in Section 5(n) has been useful. However, we are concerned that attempting to codify selected portions of the Statement might create obstacles to bringing important law enforcement actions. For example, it might undermine the Commission's efforts

---

[43] *FTC Policy Statement on Unfairness*, appended to *International Harvester Co.*, 104 F.T.C. 949, 1070 (1984), *available at* https://www.ftc.gov/public-statements/1980/12/ftc-policy-statement-unfairness.

to prevent likely substantial harm before it occurs, even though Section 5 expressly empowers and directs the Commission to <u>prevent</u> entities from engaging in unfair or deceptive acts or practices.

VI.   CONCLUSION

Thank you for the opportunity to provide the Commission's views. The FTC remains committed to finding ways to enhance its effectiveness in protecting consumers and promoting competition, to anticipate and respond to changes in the marketplace, and to meet current and future challenges. We stand ready to work with this Subcommittee as it develops and considers legislation to tackle these critical issues.